Where the Sky has No Stars

Matrika Press is proud to publish this book of poems by
Wesley Burton.

Where the Sky has No Stars

Wesley Burton

Matrika Press
Publisher

Copyright © Wesley Burton

September 2016

All Rights Reserved
including the right of reproduction,
copying, or storage in any form
or means, including electronic,
In Whole or Part,
without prior written
permission of the author

ISBN: 978-1-946088-11-6

Library of Congress Control Number: 2016916095
1.Poetry 2.Nature Poems 3.Love Poems 4. Spiritual Exploration
5.Healing Depression 6.Transcendentalism 7.Title

Matrika Press
164 Lancey Street
Pittsfield, Maine
(760) 889-5428
Editor@MatrikaPress.com

Matrika Press

www.MatrikaPress.com

First Edition
Cover art by: Barb Denaro ©
Edited by: "Twinkle" Marie Manning
Printed in the USA

"Trust thyself: every heart vibrates to that iron string."

Ralph Waldo Emerson

Dedication

*To Deborah Rozeboom,
who taught me to find my voice,
to trust it,
and to use it.*

Wesley Burton

Contents

Running with Scissors
Rain
Our Rock
Eyes Watching God
Bystander
The Sign from a Park Light
Shading Pain
Valentines
Frozen Love
My Secret Love
Karma
The Ritual of Smoking
Table in Boston
Shattering Silence
To Watch the Sun Rise
Dreaming Eyes
Rays
Small Things
Where the Sky Has No Stars
Writing
How Deep It Goes

Notes from the Poet & Publisher

Where the Sky has No Stars

Wesley Burton

Running with Scissors

Those eyes
were scolding embers
  of a summer night's fire -
fanned skyward
  by the cool breeze -
fed with night walks
and philosophy
from a yellow
bedroom window.

Thoughts
  like sparks flew
  into the night clouds -
and words,
tossed through the screen
to the chirping crickets,
and the surface of the pool
      rippled
like a dead dragon fly's wing,
caught in the swaying trees
  we prayed to.
We told our destiny
to the stars -
unscathed children -
leaving their hopes
  on the wall
of times to come -
or was it an epitaph of blue summers
and white rain under the moon
that seemed to trickle
from the stars
into my heart?

    Soon the stars descend
    and break the whispers
    and take with them the dreams
    that run with scissors.

Where the Sky has No Stars

Wesley Burton

Rain

I cannot fall
behind my eyes,
for my taunted
soul
cries
to the eves
outside my window,
as the dripping rain
calls back
a song so wild and blue -
it scrambles time
and thoughts
if it gets through to you.

Where the Sky has No Stars

Wesley Burton

Our Rock

Half emerged
in the sea -
traveled on a glacier
to stand
solid
in the waves
or dry in the sun
while foam
stuck to the surface
and clung for life.
Bubbles
drifted to sea -
we waved them goodbye
from our jagged rock
towel spot
while I traced
the curves
above your heart
ignoring the sunset's
blazing colors
and the crickets call
to watch
only you.

Where the Sky has No Stars

Wesley Burton

Eyes Watching God

When the tire rim
was filled
with scolding logs,
our feet
could be heard
crunching down the
dirt driveway
to the lightless
road
where foxes loomed
in the tall grass
peppered with peeping
crickets.
And the drone
of distant highway cars
against the silence
seemed to strum
the galaxy of
restless stars
above us.
The mystery
that lay between
the trees all around us –
barricading our path.
Eyes watching us
as our eyes
were watching God.

Where the Sky has No Stars

Wesley Burton

Bystander

The waves
  took us out
like weightless beings
chasing angels.
Silly sea birds
snatched their lowly
crumbs
against the bleak horizon
silhouetted
overhead.
  Sweating cans
of beer
poured in the sand
as he walked
  in the throbbing heat
-Pulsing as it rose-
over the sand-etchings.
His sun-glassed eyes spotted us.
I hoped
he would lose his way
and not find us,
lobster-red, in the sun,
but fate was cruel,
and lead him directly
into the hands
of the one
I loved that summer.

Where the Sky has No Stars

Wesley Burton

The Sign from a Park Light

The park light
extinguished
as it did
the night we apologized –
A sign
from my grandfather
who walked
  by our side –
in a different time
and space.
The beam
fell and righted itself upon us,
like our thoughts of each other
we could not discuss –
the staggering unknown
  we held between us.
Will the bulb rekindle?
or will the darkness
  be continuous?

Where the Sky has No Stars

Wesley Burton

Shading Pain

They say
it will be harder
in the morning.
That the dawn
will reveal
your empty heart
the same way
the darkness
hid it,
and the sun
won't feel warm
as it rises behind
the trees
as it has
so many times before
while you were growing
in their shadows.
And now your heart aches
with the thought of
sunrise.
The thought
of being awake
under the sun -
no shelter from
light upon you -
dark shadows
from snowless pines.

Where the Sky has No Stars

Wesley Burton

Valentines

Quail feathers on railroad tracks
magnolia stems in sealing wax
blue jay wings at Halifax -
visions of love's memories.

Snowshoe prints on riverside,
ice skate scrapes on hardened tides;
I think I'll take a quiet stride,
to place another heart in me.

Daffodil braids in her hair,
like the angel made of tears;
eyes like misty morning air,
love letters perched on her chair,
stuck inside a paperback.
I guess she burned them all today,
and found someone to love in some cafe.

Tarnished weeds in ivory jars,
tarnished weeds on tapestries;
garnished words from across the seas -
news that she's not coming back.

I guess I'll throw them all away,
and find someone to love, today.

Where the Sky has No Stars

Wesley Burton

Frozen Love

Is love

so shallow

as to be forgotten?

The heart -

aged and cold

will always

Unthaw.

Where the Sky has No Stars

Wesley Burton

My Secret Love

Come –
when the night
 is mellow
and when the moon
lurks
on the pond.
Daytime thoughts
of you
still steam
in the park
and on the midway
where you
left.
Cold loneliness
amongst the
rubble of stars
that once caught our eyes –
and held our destiny,
but now merely hang
above our heads – teasing.
My eyes drip
at the rubble
of their vision -
like a Van Gough -
swirls of blue
against a purple horizon
and a waking sun.
Come -
before daytime sees you
and knows of my choice
to love you again
secretly
and offer your voice
to my wounds
to seal them
for one more night.

Where the Sky has No Stars

Wesley Burton

Karma

If you ever allow
the light
of happiness
to vacate
the Stars of her eyes –
or if you've tainted
the marrow of her life –
as I have -
the stars
you once knew
to be your own dreams
will become
empty eyes
peering
  into your Schemes -
and she who warmed your heart
on the frigid nights
will turn into
  a distant scream -
fleeing away
leaving only the dust
of ashes.

Where the Sky has No Stars

Wesley Burton

The Ritual of Smoking

We light the end
of a cancerous vessel
to breathe in
its dusty shadows
rendering us
sick and old.

In denial
of Death's eager arm
ready
to snatch our
conscience.

Ash remaining
to offer
a reminder
of the temporary
beings that were
once
our vessels.

Where the Sky has No Stars

Wesley Burton

Table in Boston

The table
where we sat
a year ago
today
still harbors
our names
and our food stains.
I remember
your face
repulsed by the
metallic cigarette
smoke
caught in the
Boston air
while
thousands
of voices
talked all around,
but only ours
were heard.
And now,
just mine.

Where the Sky has No Stars

Wesley Burton

Shattering Silence

The blackness
of dawn
is upon me.
Dragged back
to the masked
adult
who
merely
stumbles
through life
but neglects
to eat
of the fruit.
Back
to the body
riddled with fear.
I think
I'll stay inside,
inside my mind,
to avoid the
laughter's sting
and the devastating
shatter of silence.

Where the Sky has No Stars

Wesley Burton

To Watch the Sun Rise

Orange billows

rise like smoke

from the blurry horizon -

Shades illuminate -

singeing the eastern sky -

 hot coals.

The sun peers over the canyon

and the embers dissever

while the luminous atmosphere

blazes to blue.

Where the Sky has No Stars

Wesley Burton

Dreaming Eyes

When you press
your face to mine
your eyes morph
into one –
giant and blue –
as pure as summer tides.
and mine –
dark brown
thick and mysterious –
as secondhand
as spring mud.
But when we pull away
reality comes into focus
and the past scrambles
to its hiding place -
your ocean-tide eyes
are now miniscule
and lost.
It was a dream I say,
to dance with you
was just a dream.

Where the Sky has No Stars

Wesley Burton

Rays

A day in the sun:
my job was
to lay the hay to sleep
around the onion stems.
My skinning knees,
speckled with soil
from kneeling
amongst the rows
of scallions.
July rays warmed
the part of my hair
when I dropped
 my baseball cap -
stained with
two generations of
summer sweat -
on the soil.
The aroma of life
all around.
Even still
after the sun
had slid behind the pines
and I had walked
two hours home
I could still
feel the warmth
of the rays
beneath my skin.

Where the Sky has No Stars

Wesley Burton

Small Things

Each time
I walk by
the magnolia tree,
I pluck a flower
and hold it in
my hands.
It reminds me
of a time
when we used to walk
the hot asphalt
of town
in the depth
of summertime,
or the cool black
sea of tar
after rain.
Talking for hours -
getting through to you
the small things
that leave a scar.
Looking at them now,
in the empty spot light,
they were
  all that mattered.

Where the Sky has No Stars

Wesley Burton

Where the Sky Has No Stars

I live
where the sky
has no stars -
where the sun
  never visits -
and time
isn't a friend.
Darkness
  rules the place
like an apocalypse.
Cliffs
have no shape -
they rest on the ground
and the sea
is fishless.
The waters -
  murky and barren.
Once -
castles ruled the land,
and gypsies
danced their messages
in the sand -
but the waves
swallowed them.
Beaded jewels
hung from clouds
And masked parties
swept the night
into the dawn
in mansions
where food
wasn't the only thing
that was catered.
Now I live where
the sky has no stars -

Where the Sky has No Stars

Wesley Burton

Where the sky Has No Stars Cont'd.

where every street
stops at a sign -
and leads
to nowhere –
this is my abode.
And when I look up,
to dream of
the majestic beauty
of castles in the sun,
I see blackness.
Nothingness.
Grabbing the sun,
stealing the blue,
tapping on the glass
to taunt me –
as I try to hide from
its clutch.
I cannot run,
because it is already
within me.

Where the Sky has No Stars

Wesley Burton

Writing

Your beauty
still stalks
the corners
of my mind.
My love for you
resides there -
a memory.
The elation of my soul
has abandoned me
like someone else
who has vanished
eternally.
But I voice my pain
in the dead of night
to the rain -
to the leaf of my journal
that drools with emotion -
my heart scribing every word -
my lonely potion.

Where the Sky has No Stars

Wesley Burton

How Deep It Goes

I heard it in the wind
cries of falling leaves
against the stray cats
and dying bees;
a time when love was blind,
or did it perceive me?

Sitting in some Café
far from home
and out of my league;
with raw sunsets
to be spent alone
with quiet,
aching tears.

Oh! How deep it goes
in the night -
the empty spotlight -
condemned to the cold white keys
and chords that I feel,
until the day flickers out,
pregnant with chance currents
of vision and pain
I tune in
once in a while
to see if you are still flowing
through my veins.

Where the Sky has No Stars

Note from the Poet

The poems in this chapbook deal with loss and depression; as they are; as I felt them. In the fall, and winter of 2014, I was sixteen and completely off my tracks. I had lost my first real love, my grandmother whom I loved more than myself, and an uncle who taught me to find my spirit through nature. Going through these mountainous conversions, poems were my way of confronting myself. I sought a greater honesty of my myself to convey what I was feeling; as it was. To get out the pen and face the beast was probably the best thing that ever happened to me. It was my first instinct when I was alone, and it was my only friend.

These poems were written at my lowest point, and they were the catalysts for my transformation. They were all I had when I felt like I had nothing. They were my thoughts, my feelings, and my life for months after several people has seemingly disappeared. This work was cathartic for me. It was the completion of a circle.

When you read the lines of these poems, I hope you can see yourself in my words. Without that self-reflection, these poems are merely ordered words meant to afflict a vision. Whether they get through to you, or whether they don't go straight to the core of your spirit, I hope you can see at least a part of yourself here, and through that, realize that you ARE NOT ALONE.

This book is dedicated to Deborah Rozeboom, who taught me to find my voice, to trust it, and to use it.

Wesley Burton.

Where the Sky has No Stars

Note from the Publisher

Matrika Press is delighted and proud to honor Wesley Burton's gift he brings to the world with his incredibly insightful poetry by publishing his first collection of poems.

Wesley's poetry reflects his deep appreciation for Nature and keen intuitions on the human experience. Contemplative and imaginative, his poetry entices readers to face moments of transition. His work explores the inner depths of the psyche, the healing power of Nature, and the soul's resilience to move forward out of darkness.

Wesley's desire to share this work with others in the hope that his words may help those faced with similar challenges demonstrates deep compassion. It is with gratitude we present to you, *"Where the Sky has No Stars."*

For more information on this wonderful emerging poet, visit: www.MatrikaPress.com/Wesley-Burton

~ The Publisher and Editors of Matrika Press

OTHER MATRIKA PRESS SELECTIONS

Seventh Principle Studies:
The 7th UU Principle is: *"Respect for the interdependent web of all existence of which we are a part."* Evidence to support such a principle is found within the pages of *The Way of Power.*

Fourth Source Explorations:
This allegorical story by David Starr Jordan is a tale about the search for spiritual meaning. Symbolic of Jesus Christ's ministry, it succinctly embodies the Unitarian Universalist Christian heritage and the fourth of the six sources we draw our faith from, namely that which calls us to respond to God's love by loving our neighbors as ourselves.

www.MatrikaPress.com

Women of Spirit

Exploring Sacred Paths of Wisdom Keepers
Compiled and Edited by "Twinkle" Marie Manning
Cover Art by Shiloh Sophia
a Sojourn With Light Workers book

This book is a compilation of women sojourners, sages, mystics, witches, shaman, medicine women, ministers, philosophers, therapists, life coaches, yogis, and more. Their journeys. Their stories. Their teachings and practices. Essays, Poetry, Art, Rituals and Prayers. This anthology is full of useful tools and powerful messages for everyone who is on a spiritual journey to embrace and enjoy. Originally published in 2014, this beautiful anthology has been recently revised and re-released. Beloved Contributors include:

- *Anna Huckabee Tull* • *Bernadette Rombough* • *Deb Elbaum*
- *Deborah Diamond* • *Debra Wilson Guttas* • *Grace Ventura*
- *Janeen Barnett* • *JoAnne Bassett* • *Judy Ann Foster*
- *Julie Matheson* • *Kate Early* • *Kate Kavanagh* • *Katherine Glass*
- *Kris Oster* • *Lea M. Hill* • *Meghan Gilroy* • *Morwen Two Feathers*
- *Rustie MacDonald* • *Shamanaca* • *Sharon Hinckley* • *Shawna Allard*
- *Shiloh Sophia* • *Susan Feathers* • *Tiffany Cano* • *Tory Londergan*
- *"Twinkle" Marie Manning* • *Tziporah Kingsbury* • *Valerie Sorrentino*

RECOMMENDED SELECTIONS FROM CHB MEDIA

CHB MEDIA POETRY ANTHOLOGIES —
Including the poetry of Twinkle Marie Manning

Poetry to Feed the Spirit
A Contemporary Anthology
of Central Florida Poets, Volume 1

Love & Other Passions
A Contemporary Anthology
of Central Florida Poets, Volume 2

Buy online at chbmediaonline.com, amazon.com, or barnesandnoble.com

COMING SOON:

Therese's Dream – Maine to Darfur: A Doctor's Story, chronicles Dr. David Austin's time with Doctors Without Borders and illustrates the common humanity of peoples around the world.

Dr. Austin is a lifelong Unitarian Universalist who has dedicated his life to healing and service.

www.MatrikaPress.com/dr-david-austin

Should you wish to Publish your work, visit our website for submission guidelines. Please note: As an independent publisher, we *do* accept unsolicited manuscripts at this time.

www.MatrikaPress.com

RECOMMENDED SELECTIONS FROM SKINNER HOUSE

Finding the Voice Inside: *Writing As a Spiritual Quest for Women*
Gail Collins-Ranadive offers forty practical and imaginative writing exercises that invite women to explore their uniquely feminine spirituality. Through writing of symbols, metaphors and truths of their own lives, women re-awaken to higher truths of their sacredness.

Reaching for the Sun
Rev. Angela Herrera's book of meditations, prayers and invocations provide inspiration to readers and serve as a resource to those seeking powerful liturgical words, grounded in the experiences of everyday life.

Evening Tide
This book of mediations by Elizabeth Tarbox helps readers to face the darker moments of life, the challenging circumstances that call us to live more fully even when we feel our most empty.

http://www.uua.org/publications/skinnerhouse

RECOMMENDED SELECTIONS FROM BEACON PRESS

Claiming the Spirit Within
This wonderful book, edited by Rev. Marilyn Sewell, is a beautiful sourcebook of poetry and prose. A rich and diverse anthology dedicated to the praise of life, it presents the sacredness that emerges when women immerse fully in living lives of spirit while embracing the physical. Its contents include more than 300 poems celebrating all aspects of women's lives. Contributors include Margaret Atwood, Rita Dove, Louise Erdrich, Tess Gallagher, Nikki Giovanni, Joy Harjo, and Maxine Hong Kingston.

A Chosen Faith: *An Introduction to Unitarian Universalism*
Authored by Forrest Church and John A. Buehrens, this book offers a an informative look at Unitarian Universalism. The authors explore the history and sources of this living tradition. For those contemplating religious choices, Unitarian Universalism offers an appealing alternative to religious denominations that stress theological creeds over individual conviction and belief. It allows room for individual interpretations of the sacred and encourages affirming diversity, personal choice, shared experiences, rites of passage, religious education and work for social justice.

http://www.beacon.org/

ISBN 978-1-946088-11-6
50999